DETAILS

www.oldmatemedia.com

First Published in 2020 by Old Mate Media.

Written and Edited by: Chris Stead
Designed by: Chris Stead
Published by: Old Mate Media
ISBN Hardcover: 978-1-925638-78-3
ISBN Paperback: 978-1-925638-77-6

Text and Images Copyright © 2020 Old Mate Media, except those images supplied freely by companies for the promotion of their games. No text or images may be reproduced wholly or in part in any form of media without prior written permission from the creators, Chris Stead and Kate Stead, of Old Mate Media. The entire contents of this book are the copyright of Old Mate Media except the aforementioned images relating to the promotion of games by third-party companies. This book is meant as a guide only.

First Edition

CONTENTS

Introducing the PlayStation 5..4

The PS5 Hardware...5

Instant Loading..8

3D Audio Explained...9

The Problem of Storage..11

PS5 vs PS5 Digital Edition..12

Understanding the DualSense controller..13

Backwards Compatibility on the PS5...16

PS5 Peripherals...18

Sony Reinvents its User Interface..22

Looking at Design...24

What is PlayStation Plus?..26

The Bottom Line...28

Where to Buy a PS5..30

The Best Launch Games on PS5?...31

What does the future look like for PS5?...61

Also Out..63

INTRODUCING THE PLAYSTATION 5

Sony comes into the ninth generation of video gaming in a great position. First releasing in November 2013, the PS4 powered its way to approximately 112 million worldwide sales. The result saw it finish its race as the second most successful console of all time, behind only the 155 million selling PS2. Perhaps more importantly, it dwarfed the 50 million consoles of its main rival, the Xbox One.

As such, in 2020 Sony has all the momentum ahead of the launch of the PS5. It has the fans. It has the most popular exclusives and franchises. And it has a strong position with which to negotiate better opportunities with third-party developers and retailers.

Yet the Japanese giant hasn't played it safe. Indeed, the PlayStation 5 takes some significant gambles, looking to overhaul the user-interface, controller, role of backwards compatibility and storage solutions. This isn't the same experience fans have become accustomed to, but is it better? Change is always a risk; will Sony reap the reward? Will gamers?

In this guide, I'll take you through everything you need to know about the PlayStation 5. What is Sony's view on the next generation of gaming and how does that fit with the experience you want to play? What are the best games on the new console? And how does the PlayStation 5 separate itself from Microsoft's rival Xbox Series X console?

Let's find out.

THE PS5 HARDWARE

It's been seven years since Sony launched the PS4 and, as you can imagine, technology has changed significantly in that time. Even though we saw mid-generation releases such as the PS4 Pro up the ante on what gamers could experience, that system was still confined by the limitations its lesser brothers. With a new generation comes the chance to truly start fresh; gamers expect a significant boost in power.

And they get it. For those of you who are tech minded, I will share the raw specifications. But don't worry, I will go into greater detail about what it means in a tick.

PS5 Specifications

CPU: 8-core AMD Zen 2, 3.5 GHz variable frequency
Power: 10.28 teraflops
GPU: Custom AMD RDNA 2-based GPU
Storage: NVMe M.2 825GB SSD hard drive at 5.5GB/s to 9GB/s read speed
Memory: 16GB GDDR6 256-bit with 448GB/s bandwidth
Controller: DualSense, PSVR
Features: 3D audio, ray-tracing, 8K ready, HDMI 2.1
Dimensions: 26cm (d) × 10.4cm (w) × 39cm (h)
Weight: 4.5kg

The PS5 brings with it 10.28 teraflops of power. That's just under 10 times the power of the PS4's 1.84 teraflops and significantly more than the PS4 Pro's 4.2 teraflops. It is, however, considerably less than the Xbox Series X, which offers 12.13 teraflops of power.

On paper, this places the PlayStation 5 at a disadvantage when compared to the Xbox Series X. But there is more to the conversation than just teraflops; the devil is in the details. Sony has taken an all-in approach with its CPU and memory, offering a single capped speed for each of these components regardless of the actions being performed. Microsoft, on the other hand, has multiple speeds for CPU and memory based on how they are being utilised.

This empowers the argument that the distance between the two isn't as great as it seems on paper, because how often is the XSX using all its power?

Sony also has a major advantage with is storage solution. Its NVMe M.2 825GB internal hard drive is effectively twice the speed of the storage solution offered in the Xbox Series X. Sony argues that power is irrelevant if the hardware can't access the content quickly. The company suggests that while the XSX has more power, it's bottlenecked by its slow hard drive. Whereby, the PS5 can leverage all its power thanks to its faster hard drive.

Microsoft of course begs to differ, saying it has other technology on its machine – namely the Xbox Velocity Architecture – that helps improve the communication between hardware and software in such a way the read speed of the HD becomes irrelevant. Who are you going to believe?

The reality is it could all be a moot point in the end; at least for a couple of years. Both the Xbox Series X and the PlayStation 5 boast incredibly fast load times of games and can display titles at 60 frames-per-second in 8K resolution. This is a visual standard – and therefore power demand – that we're years away from needing on a regular basis. At least general gamers with general TVs and expectations.

Why? Because if you don't have an HDMI 2.1 input port on your TV, you cannot get that top-end resolution. You can't even get 120fps on a 4K game without a HDMI 2.1 port. Most gamers will be capped at HDMI 2.0 speeds regardless of the PS5's power, and that maxes out at 60fps at 4K.

So, what will Sony's faith in its hard drive ultimately deliver? Over time, we may see large open-world experiences being able to display slightly bigger and more immersive worlds than we see on XSX. Maybe. Only time will tell.

Before we move on, it's worth mentioning the cooling fan in the PS5. Sony's new console is the biggest console of all time and in large part this is due to the huge cooling fan. The noise of the fan in the PS4 was one of the console's biggest issues, and with all the added power, an even bigger fan was required for the PS5.

However, the fan is adaptive. Its software can be updated over time not just as an all-or-nothing change, but to match the needs of specific games. This will allow it to behave as required, and certainly initial tests with the console suggest the PS5 is very quiet in operation.

Hooray!

INSTANT LOADING

It seems like fast loading would be way down the pecking order when considering the best features of the PS5 hardware, but it's not. On the contrary, it's one of the most exciting changes to the way we can expect to play in the next generation. (That extends to the Xbox Series X, which also features similar accelerated load speeds.)

With the previous generation of consoles, loading into a game was incredibly painful. Sometimes it could take multiple minutes to go from wanting to play a game to it actually loading. While that was painful, it got even worse if you wanted to switch between different games during any given gaming session.

Those days are dead.

Games now load in a matter of seconds. It's not instant (despite what the marketing gurus at Sony will tell you), but it's near painless. At least with the initial run of games. As the generation continues and games get bigger, perhaps even starting to offer 8K resolutions, then there will be more to load, and the idea of "instant loading" may be lost. But at this stage, being able to jump straight into a game feels amazing.

The ability to fast load also ties into the ability to have multiple games paused at any single time. I will go into more detail about this feature when we discuss the user interface.

3D AUDIO EXPLAINED

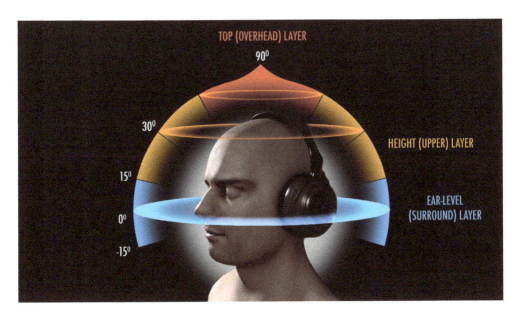

One of the more interesting features of the PS5 is the way its handling next-generation sound. Where Microsoft has stuck with the industry standard in Dolby Atmos, Sony has created its own sound engine called Tempest, which delivers an experience called 3D Audio.

3D Audio goes a step further than surround sound. Instead of surrounding your head with sounds based on where your headset or speakers are placed, 3D Audio puts the listener in the middle of a 3D space and makes them the pivot point. I realise that's a hard description to understand, but perhaps this example will help it make more sense.

With Dolby Atmos, the sound moves with your head. Turn your head to the left and the sound doesn't change. It's still just surrounding your ears as it did before. 3D Audio, however, understands that your head has turned and changes the sound accordingly. So what was once beside you may now be behind you.

But that's just the start. As you move through a game world, it also understands that the objects in that world and your proximity to them are also playing a role in the way sound is bouncing around. Or absorbed. It understands that the sound should therefore hit your ears in a different fashion now that you've, for example, taken a step forward into a room.

Hundreds of different sounds and the way they should travel through any given space in any given moment are simulated simultaneously, which creates a much more immersive experience. Especially when playing in VR! And in good news, while 3D Audio compatible headphones, soundbars and home theatres will make the most of this feature, standard audio setups – even your TV speakers – will benefit from 3D Audio.

Let's just hope developers make a genuine effort to build games that make use of 3D Audio! I've heard demos of rain failing where you feel like you can hear every individual drop hitting a unique surface and it's stunning.

THE PROBLEM OF STORAGE

Opting to go with such a tip-of-the-spear storage solution may end up being the hardware decision that makes the PS5 shine, but it comes at a cost. The internal hard drive has just 825GB of storage, which is pathetic. Even less than the current PS4.

To put that storage quota in context, the ultimate edition of launch title Marvel's Spider-Man: Miles Morales requires a 106GB install. While that may end up being on the larger side, you're still looking at only a handful of games being installed on the internal hard drive at any one time. Sony has made it clear that if you want to get the full PS5 experience from your PS5 games, you need to do so with its NVMe M.2 SSD hard drive, too.

That means you can't just plug an external hard drive, install your games on it, and expect them to run at PS5 standards. They'll run well enough to play, but you'll be making sacrifices with load times and potentially resolution and/or framerate. You can expand the internal hard drive, of course. In fact, the two white sails that cup the console clip off quite easily. But it's not cheap.

I feel that increasing hard drive space is one of the bigger immediate "hidden costs" next-generation gamers will face. But you could be looking at spending an additional $200 to $400 in order to get the hard drive capacity you need if you want to have a dozen or more blockbuster games played at any one time.

PS5 VS PS5 DIGITAL EDITION

Sony is launching the PS5 in two forms; the stock PS5 and the PS5 Digital Edition. It's important to note that under the hood, both machines are identical. There is no difference in power. However, the Digital Edition is lacking an optical Blu-ray drive. No doubt you've picked that up simply by looking at the two machines side-by-side. One clearly doesn't have disc drive, sporting a tighter, more svelte figure as a result.

It goes without saying then that with the PlayStation 5 Digital Edition, you cannot play Blu-ray movies or CDs, or indeed even the discs of backwards compatible PS4 games. It's not a big loss; not nowadays. Most consumers now stream their movie and music media rather than use a disc after all.

I'm hesitant to mention prices in this guide given that you could be reading this book from anywhere in the world, but in my opinion, the PS5 Digital Edition is a worthy consideration. You'll save around 20% on the price of a PS5. In the USA, the premium PS5 is US$499 and the Digital Edition is US$399, for example. Is it really worth the extra money for a disc drive that's already out-of-date?

It's worth noting that having a disc drive does not save you storage space in any significant way. You will still need to install your game on the hard drive, whether you have a disc or download the game from the internet.

With that in mind, you may be wondering who would consider the fully featured PS5. The answer likely lies in gamers who live in an area where internet speeds are poor. Waiting for a 100GB game to download may simply be too painful if a disc can be purchased and played near instantly. The other demographic will be gamers who intend on bargain hunting for games at markets, garage sales or at retailers who specialise in pre-owned titles.

UNDERSTANDING THE DUALSENSE CONTROLLER

The days of the DualShock are over. PlayStation's iconic controller has been with us since the mid-90s, but after four generations it has been retired. In its stead comes the DualSense. At a distance the controller may not look like that big of a change from what we've seen for years, but don't be fooled. The DualSense plays a huge role in putting the next in next-generation gaming.

Sony has looked to truly innovate here. With the power of the PS5 able to deliver a visual and auditory experience beyond most modern home theatre setups, it was a case of where-to-next in the hunt for complete gamer immersion. Sony has fallen to the device in our hands to take that next leap.

The DualSense is, of course, functional. But it's also a conduit through which a game's world becomes more tangible; more real. It does this through four key features:

1. **Haptic Feedback:** This is the next generation of the old Rumble feature we've seen in previous console controllers. Haptic sensors offer far more detailed feedback than Rumble. They can be activated in multiple zones of the controller at once, and at different pressures, too. It feels incredible in your hands, really adding to the game experience.

In Spider-Man, for example, when you throw an electric punch, you can feel the bolt fizzle from one side of the controller to the other. In Astro's Playroom, you can tell what material the character is walking on from the feel of the vibrations.

Meanwhile, in Deathloop, if your gun jams, you can feel the violence of the kickback in the palm of your hand. And that can be different for each gun. You get the idea.

2. **Adaptive Triggers:** Previously, when you pulled a trigger on your controller, the pressure you needed to apply was the same no matter what the action. That's not the case anymore. Depending on what you are trying to do in a game, the effort you will need to use to squeeze the trigger will change.

For example, trying to pull back the string of a bow requires more effort the further you draw. Or if a gun jams, you will suddenly not be able to pull back the trigger easily at all. It's a stunning addition that really enhances your gaming experience.

3. **Touchpad:** While not a new feature – it appeared in the DualShock 4 – the touchpad has been improved so it's more accessible. Its rounder shape and larger profile make it easier to access quickly with a thumb while playing. Hopefully this will encourage more developers to make better use of it in their games, but it's still a boon when interacting with the UI.

4. **Mic:** The built-in microphone means you can talk to your game, or more often other players in an online multiplayer experience, without a headset. Simply talk and the microphone on the controller will pick it up and do the work for you. This makes communication on the PS5 much more user-friendly, but also opens the door to voice commands becoming more prevalent in games and in the UI.

Elsewhere, the light bar of the PS4 has been scaled back. It still exists, but it now sits under the touchpad, making it far more subtle. There is also now a Create button, which is how players will not just share content (such as video of their gameplay or screenshots) but edit that media. While the speakers in the controller itself are much improved.

Unfortunately, all this goodness comes at a price. You can expect to pay 20% more for a DualSense than you did a DualShock. While that isn't the end of the world, unlike the Xbox Series X, old PS4 controllers will not work on the console. At least, not with new games. We'll go into backwards compatibility in more detail later, but if you want to play a PS5 game in co-op with a friend of sibling, you're going to need a second DualSense controller.

In the positive, the DualSense is rechargeable. So, unlike the Xbox Series X controller, you're not going to have go through bucketloads of environmentally unfriendly batteries to play. Just plug it into a wall or into the DualSense Charging Dock.

BACKWARDS COMPATIBILITY ON THE PS5

The choice by Sony to forge ahead with a console that feels new and futuristic has had some unfortunate side effects. Namely, the new machine isn't that great with its backwards compatibility.

Whereas the Xbox Series X can play games from all previous Xbox consoles natively on the machine, the PS5 is less giving. PS3, PS2, Vita, PSP and PSOne games will not work on the PS5 at all. And while the vast majority of PS4 games will be backwards compatible eventually, they'll achieve compatibility in a more drip-fed fashion.

They also don't get an automatic boost from the added power. Unless patched by the developer, backwards compatible PS4 games will effectively be emulated on a PS5 as they originally were experienced.

If patched, however, Game Boost can kick up the resolution and framerate of old games, as well as help them load faster. But it remains a mystery as to whether your favourite game will get that treatment or be left to their original form.

It's a bit disappointing, especially when you consider that the backwards compatibility issues extend to some of the hardware. The DualShock 4 controllers of the PS4 era will sync with a PS5 and can be used to play backwards compatible PS4 games. However, a DualShock can't be used to play PS5 games.

The PS4 PlayStation camera is also not backwards compatible out of the box. Thankfully, you can get a PS Camera adaptor from Sony for free, but the details on how to do that weren't revealed at the time of writing. To add to the frustration, while the PSVR headset is backwards compatible, you can't use it with the new PS5 HD Camera. Argh! At least if you already have a PS4 camera, you don't need to upgrade.

Elsewhere, there's less confusion. Existing headsets from Sony and third-party hardware makers will continue to work on the PS5 without the user needing to do anything. As will the now decade-old PlayStation Move controllers and advanced peripherals such as the Logitech G steering wheel.

Backwards compatibility certainly isn't as straightforward and user-friendly as we hoped for with the PS5, but its impact on you may be minimal. Are you likely to play couch multiplayer and require a second DualSense controller? Do you care about playing old games or are you only interested in new titles?

How do cross-generation games work?

One of the key features Microsoft is touting with its XSX console is Smart Delivery. Effectively this means that if you buy a cross-generation game, you'll download the version that is relevant to your console at no extra cost. For example, if you buy Dirt 5 on XBO and then get an XSX, you can just download the newer version for free.

This philosophy isn't mandated by Microsoft, but it's heavily leaned on when it comes down to cross-generation games.

Sony offers the same feature. The company just hasn't given it an official name and has instead left next-generation upgrades in the hands of developers. For most cross-generation games, if you get the PS4 version, you can upgrade to the PS5 version at no cost (well, outside of Internet costs in downloading additional content).

It's worth pointing out that there is nothing specifically different between the content of these cross-generation games between consoles. Instead, the PS5 versions make explicit use of the DualSense controller and offer an improved visual and audio experience.

Just keep in mind that cross-generation upgrades only work for digital versions of PS4 games if you have a PS5 Digital Edition console – not boxed games. So, if you're thinking of getting one of the PS4's blockbusters and upgrading to a PS5 version down the track, make sure you buy it online.

PS5 PERIPHERALS

Depending on what kind of experience you are looking for from your PlayStation 5, there are a host of peripherals you may wish to grab. Here's an overview of the official extras you can consider.

DualSense Controller

The most likely addition most people will need to add to their PS5 purchase is an additional DualSense controller. We go into more detail on what this controller offers elsewhere in the guide, but if you intend to play PS5 games in local multiplayer – be it competitive or co-op – then you need a second DualSense. You cannot play PS5 games with a PS4 controller.

The DualSense isn't cheap either, but they are a quality piece of futuristic technology that really does improve the user experience.

DualSense Controller Charging Station

If you've got multiple DualSense controllers, you may also want to consider a Charging Station. This holds two controllers at once in a neat little dock, allowing them to charge via any USB port you've got access to. This becomes particularly handy if you have external hard drives or other peripherals, like PSVR, that want to take up USB ports on your PS5. Instead of always having two USBs taken up by controller cables, you can offload all the work to the Charging Station.

PS5 Media Remote

If you intend to turn your PlayStation 5 into the main media hub of your lounge room, then you can upscale that experience with the Media Remote. Note, you don't need this device; you can just use your DualSense controller. But that's not a great experience. This remote is specifically designed to work with the Blu-ray player and streaming apps like Netflix, do does a better job.

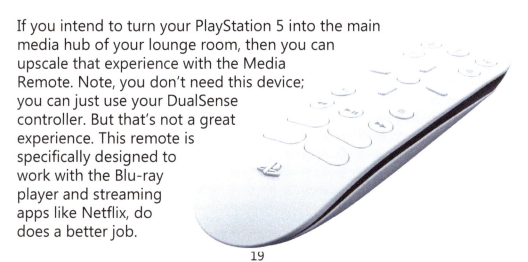

Sony Pulse 3D Wireless Headset

Make no mistake, if you don't have a good audio solution then you are missing out on half the gaming experience. Sound is so vital to genuine immersion and will actually improve your play by giving you better spatial awareness. Especially in multiplayer! The PS5 utilises 3D Audio, a new feature that looks to one-up the Dolby Atmos experience offered by the Xbox Series X.

There are plenty of home theatre systems and soundbars out there that will offer you a pretty good 3D Audio experience, but if you need a different solution, then going with this official headset is a smart call. It's specifically built to make the most of the PS5's 3D Audio and Sony itself has been a leader in headset technology for decades.

It comes with a rechargeable battery that delivers around 12-hours of wireless play and is also compatible with PCs and Macs. It's competitively priced, too.

PS5 HD Camera

The new PS5 camera is built with streaming in mind. It comes with a built-in background remover for starters, allowing you to broadcast yourself over the game as you play. The camera delivers a 1080p stream, which is solid without being spectacular, but it does feature two wide-angle lenses to ensure you can get a good shot in a small room.

Perhaps more importantly, at least during the launch window you cannot use the new PS5 HD Camera with the PlayStation VR headset. The older PS4 era camera, combined with an adaptor, must be used. So, if VR is part of the PS5's future, there must be a big update to the headset coming sometime soon.

PlayStation VR

While Sony hasn't updated the technology in its PSVR headset for the PS5 console, it remains a killer addition to your gaming experience. Playing games in VR is such a mind-blowing experience and there's no shortage of great games already available in the PlayStation ecosystem. Just be careful to lookout for a bundle that includes the new the old PS4-era PlayStation camera along with a PS5 adaptor. The new PS5 camera does not work with the headset.

SONY REINVENTS ITS USER INTERFACE

Sony isn't just looking to iterate on the PS4 with the PS5; it's looking to provide something fresh, innovative and even futuristic. This is evidenced in the hardware choices, the DualSense controller, and also in the user interface (UI). Where Microsoft has left the UI of the XSX more-or-less the same as what we saw in the latter stages of the Xbox One's lifecycle, Sony has started from scratch.

The PS5 dashboard features a user interface that still feels very much like a Sony product. However, at every turn it offers something far more integrated, organic and as such, user-friendly. It allows you to spend more time in the game and less time in the menus.

Starting with the home screen, you no longer flip through various menus to get all the information you need around a game. Simply scroll to the game and everything you need to know about it instantly appears. This includes a purchase button, shared content from other users, tips on how to play and more. This full integration of the Store into the browsing experience is a simple, but fantastic change.

Not that you need to head to the home screen to interact with the interface while playing a game. On the PS5, you can bring up the UI over your game, allowing you to interact with friends, join up with party members or even jump to different mods or levels with ease.

A particularly cool feature allows you to overlay video content in a picture-in-picture style scenario that can play as you're gaming. This is best realised by the help videos that appear when you tap out to the UI. You can watch these in real-time in a small window while you play on the bigger window. What a great way to get past difficult areas without offering any spoilers! Alternatively you can watch a stream of your friend as they play, even if it's a different game.

When you bring up the UI over a game you are playing, these options are presented as customisable cards that overlay the action. Some of these cards are called PlayStation Activities, which are shortcuts that can jump you to certain sections of a game instantly. For example, you could jump straight into your favourite multiplayer mode. Or to a quest you have not completed. Or to your favourite level.

Ultimately, these Activities will be defined by the developer, but there is no doubting that the ease of access invites gamers to experience more out of their games. It's worth noting that you don't have to stick to the one game, either. You can have multiple games running at once and simply switch between them, continuing to play exactly where you left off during your last session. So futuristic!

Speaking of futuristic, or at least from the perspective of a video game console, you can also now issue voice commands directly through your DualSense controller to the PS5. This works in a similar fashion to what you may have seen in certain smart TVs. Holding down the mic button can allow you to say a word you want to search, for example, rather than type it.

Of course, we expect the PS5 user interface to get better as the generation continues. Regular patches should ensure that Sony starts with this fantastic UI foundation and builds on it over the years.

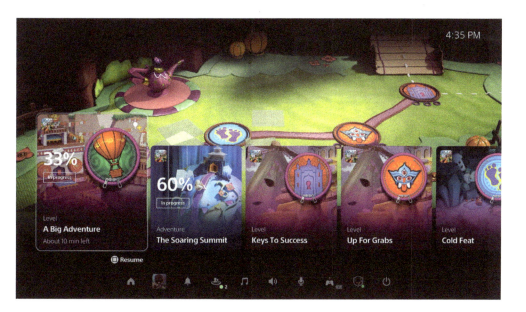

LOOKING AT DESIGN

I'll admit, it's taken me a while to warm to the design of the PlayStation 5. Like the rest of the console, Sony hasn't taken the safe route with its new design. The PS5 not only looks a lot different to Sony's previous consoles, but any other console in history. It's also huge; the biggest console ever made. It makes its clam-like design, with top and bottom sails cupping the main console, even more dominant in your lounge room.

Yet warm to it I have. The sails, or upper and lower lips if you like, are covered with fine little PlayStation emblems, giving it a much more textured (and expensive) feel when you get up, close and personal. While the way it lights up and its modern, white finish do make it pop when sat next to the other technology around your TV. It achieves its goal of feeling futuristic.

In my opinion, the console looks best when horizontal, but you can stand it vertically if you like. Just remember at 40cm tall, it won't fit between shelves in a standard entertainment unit when upright.

The front panel features both a USB Type-A and one USB-C port, both offering superfast 10GB/s transfer speeds. On the back you'll find another two USB-A ports, an ethernet port and an HDMI 2.1 port. That's it. There's no second optical audio port this time around, which may cause some conflict with existing home theatre setups. Audio can only be connected via HDMI.

One interesting aspect of the design is that the white sails can be removed. They clip off relatively easily. Why would you do this? The main reason will be to add additional hard drive space in the future, but it's also likely that you will be able to customise the outer body of your PS5 with new skins in the future. Not that any were revealed before launch.

The HDMI 2.1 upgrade

As mentioned, the PS5 (and the XSX for that matter) features an HDMI 2.1 port, the latest generation of video output. It's a big upgrade from the HDMI 2.0 most of us were using at the end of the last generation. Why? It's capable of handling 48GB of data per second, as opposed to 18GB/sec with the HDMI 2.0 cables. That means more data can be transferred, allowing for better picture quality.

HDMI 2.0, for example, can only deliver 4K gameplay at 60 frames-per-second. Whereas HDMI 2.1 can deliver 4K gameplay at 120 frames-per-second, as well as 8K in 60 frames-per-second. Not only that, HDMI 2.1 can offer a great range of colours, dynamic HDR lighting and variable refresh rate (VRR) support. In short, it can produce a much better, much smoother, visual experience.

The catch, of course, is that you need a TV with an HDMI 2.1 port ready to receive this signal. Such technology isn't widespread; indeed the top of the range LG TV I bought in 2019 didn't have it (curse it!) So not too many games will be trying to reach the upper resolution and framerate limits in the initial launch years.

The question becomes whether you can live in the knowledge that you're not getting the optimal experience. If you can't live with that, it's time to upgrade your TV.

WHAT IS PLAYSTATION PLUS?

Like the Xbox and Nintendo Switch, if you want to play the PlayStation online, you're going to need to pay for an additional subscription. The service is called PlayStation Plus and while it is an additional expense, it's one that's well worth it.

Prices differ depending on where you live, but if you use the American price of US$59.99/year as a guide, you'll have a good idea of how much you will need to invest. It works out to about the same as a cup of coffee per month no matter where you live.

For that money you will get unlimited online play, access to exclusive DLC, deals on the PlayStation Store, the ability to share your own content with friends online and 100GB of online save game storage. You also get at least two free games a month to download and play for as long as you keep the membership.

These are frequently big-name blockbuster titles, too, and these two freebies alone justify the subscription's cost. It was also announced just before launch that the delayed Destruction AllStars game would be available for free on PS Plus when released in February.

PlayStation Plus Collection

There is another bonus in the mix as well. Sony has made 18 games available for free to PlayStation Plus subscribers for the launch of the new console. They are all backwards compatible PS4 games; they're not PS5 games. But they are great games, and it's an excellent way to ensure you have plenty of games to play over the initial months of console ownership.

The 18 games included as part of the PlayStation Plus Collection are; Batman: Arkham Knight, Battlefield 1, Bloodborne, Days Gone, Detroit: Become Human, Fallout 4, Final Fantasy 15, God of War, Infamous Second Son, Monster Hunter World, Mortal Kombat X, Persona 5, Ratchet and Clank, Resident Evil 7: Biohazard, The Last Guardian, The Last of Us Remastered, Uncharted 4: A Thief's End and Until Dawn.

To be fair, there isn't a dud in the list. Well, maybe Days Gone.

THE BOTTOM LINE

Sony has been much more aggressive than Microsoft in this ninth generation of consoles with respect to trying something new. Unlike its rival, the PS5 isn't iterative; it's a genuine attempt to bring gaming into a future we haven't experienced before. Personally, I commend Sony for taking that risk and looking to boldly go where no console has gone before.

By starting from scratch with the DualSense controller and the user interface, while positioning a lightning fast internal hard drive as the beating heart of its hardware, the PS5 feels next-gen. It feels futuristic. As soon as it's in your hands, you're in awe.

But it comes at the cost of accessibility. While the price of the PS5 meets that of the Xbox Series X and the Digital Edition is a very compelling and cheaper alternative, there's hidden costs that can't be ignored.

DualSense controllers, while awesome, are expensive and the internal hard drive space significantly limited. While the move to a new type of experience has hampered backwards compatibility support not just with games, but also with hardware. And while PlayStation has virtual reality in its corner, Microsoft's Game Pass and xCloud offerings may end up being more pertinent needs for gamers in this generation.

Ultimately, fans and newcomers alike are in for a fantastic experience with the PlayStation 5. It's a console that chose to aim high and it hits the mark.

The Epic Games x Sony deal

Microsoft gained a lot of attention prior to the release of the next-generation consoles when it bought behemoth third-party publisher Bethesda (and in doing so, all its technology and game IP). But Sony also made a significant play. A US$250m stake in Epic Games.

Epic Games is arguably the biggest non-console making company in the games industry. It has created some of the biggest games in history, including Unreal Tournament, Gears of War and Fortnite, and it also owns Rocket League. But it's not the software that makes Epic Games such a big deal.

Epic Games is the creator of Unreal Engine, the middleware solution that powers a huge number of games from the biggest blockbusters through to the smallest indies. Epic also owns its own PC gaming store, which is a genuine rival to Valve's Steam platform. Finally, Epic has been proactive on the blockchain front, working with cutting edge technology to improve the backend infrastructure of everything from online gaming to marketplace royalties.

While Sony's stake in the company only amounts to 1.4% of its estimated value, it does ensure a close partnership with Epic Games moving forward. Indeed, Epic Games chose the PS5 to show off its latest Unreal Engine 5 capabilities. Considering how powerful Epic Games is in the construction and distribution of gaming IP, this partnership should help Sony's chances of making continued strides with the PS5 throughout this generation.

WHERE TO BUY A PS5

Who could have predicted that the next generation of consoles would release in the middle of a global pandemic? There's no doubt that the arrival of a disease that's infected the whole world has impacted not just in stock availability, but also access to retail outlets.

While your typical department stores and specialist gaming shops will be selling the PS5, the lion's share of available stock will be going through online retailers. After all, this limits face-to-face interaction and the risk of spreading the virus. Even then though, stock is expected to be quite short through 2020 and into the start of 2021, with demand seemingly outstripping supply.

Your best bet is to stick with your bigger, global online retailers such as Amazon. Not only will they have access to more stock, but can deliver quicker shipping time when stock arrives, not to mention pre-order opportunities is stock falls short.

The only exception is if you plan to trade-in your old console, in which case heading into a physical retailer may be required.

At the time of writing, I've yet to see any particularly compelling bundle offers. But you may wish to keep your eyes out for opportunities to grab a couple of games, or important peripherals, with your console to try and save some money.

THE BEST LAUNCH GAMES ON PS5?

For many gamers, the decision on what console to buy at the start of a new generation comes down to one thing; games. After all, that's what we're here to do right? Play games.

Many of the big games launching alongside, or very near, the PlayStation 5 are multiformat titles and are also available on the Xbox Series X. They're not the titles that are going to sway you one way or the other. Instead it's the exclusive titles only available on PS5 that help the console standout from its competition.

Sony has a long history of delivery quality first-party exclusives. While this is the first generation where Microsoft has more internal studios working on games than Sony, the former has a long way to go to prove it can consistently delivery the quality and diversity of exclusive experiences Sony is renowned for.

Plus, Sony has strong ties with the biggest names of Japanese game development – Sega, Konami, Namco, Square Enix - and those relationships often deliver additional exclusives.

Indeed, when we look at the launch window games, Sony has more exclusives than Microsoft, and they're more compelling. But there's no shortage of exciting third-party titles, too. Let's take a look at the best games of the launch window. Just note the following classification guidelines as you read each page. I've put them alongside each game to help you make a better decision on what to play.

Age Range = All, Teen or Adult
Multiplayer = Yes (Local or Online)
Developer = Who made the game
Genre = A broad summation of the kind of gameplay experience

ASSASSIN'S CREED: VALHALLA

Age Range = Adult | **Multiplayer** = No
Developer = Ubisoft Montreal | **Genre** = Action

Adult gamers looking for a deep, immersive world to jump into with no shortage of action can start and stop their search with Assassin's Creed: Valhalla. The twelfth main instalment in the series and 22nd overall, Assassin's Creed needs little introduction. It transports you to a tumultuous period in Earth's history and puts you in the shoes of an assassin. You're then tasked with doing your bit to counter the Templars and play political puppet with the times.

As its title suggests, this instalment has a Viking theme. As Viking raider Eivor, you play out a mythical Norse invasion of Britain in the year 873 AD. Expect a massive open-world to explore – on foot, beast or via longboat - with a host of sidequests surrounding core story missions. Stealth plays a major role in gameplay, but combat is frequent and has been given extra depth thanks to new weapons, dual-wielding and gear with randomly generated attributes.

ASTRO'S PLAYROOM

Age Range = All | **Multiplayer** = No
Developer = Sony ASOBI Team | **Genre** = Platformer

This isn't a game you have to worry about buying; it comes pre-installed on every PS5. If you have the console; you have the game. It could be considered something of a tech demo in that respect as it's designed to show off all the features of the new DualSense controller. So expect to do plenty of activities that take the Haptic Feedback, Adaptive Triggers, Mic and Speaker through their paces.

However, it is more than a tech demo. It does offer a full platformer experience to complete. If you set your expectations to the worlds of classic Mario or Crash Bandicoot games, you will have a good idea of what to expect. Right down to the bright colours and tonnes of collectables. It's also a sequel of sorts to excellent VR game Astro Bot Rescue Mission, starring as it does the same cute little robot character. But it doesn't feature any VR itself.

BUGSNAX

Age Range = All | **Multiplayer** = No
Developer = Young Horses | **Genre** = Adventure

If you ever played Young Horses first hit, Octodad: Deadliest Catch, you'll know the developer likes to keep things light, breezy and never far from a laugh. This PS5 exclusive is one for younger gamers, filled with characters that are reminiscent of Viva Piñata crossed with The Muppets.

You play a journalist who arrives on a mysterious island paradise tasked with using a range of various traps to track down and catch bugs. The local people then snack upon the, turning them into bug snacks (get it?) As you explore you begin to unravel a bigger story around some Bugsnax that have gone missing.

The game is played from the first-person perspective and is focused on exploration, light platforming and puzzle solving. There are over 100 species of Bugsnax to discover on your journey, too, but sadly the game can only be played solo. Still, a good option for the kids.

COD BLACK OPS: COLD WAR

Age Range = Adults | **Multiplayer** = Yes (Local and Online)
Developer = Treyarch / Raven Software | **Genre** = FPS

For the best part of two decades, Call of Duty has ruled the roost when it comes to online multiplayer experiences and that's not about to change for the PS5. This is the 17th game in the series and the sixth to wield the Black Ops name. And as the name suggests, the story takes you to the Cold War, circa early 1980s. The tale is inspired by real events, taking gamers to East Berlin, Vietnam, Turkey and Russia as you, a CIA officer, track down a spy.

While the campaign is a brutal single player experience, most gamers will come for the multiplayer. An increase in game modes and customisation options build on the already solid template. A new Fireteam mode is a standout, providing a fresh 40-player mode to dive into. Zombies mode returns, too, and offers local co-op play. While the gear unlocked in this game will carry across to the now separate Warzone experience.

CYBERPUNK 2077

Age Range = Adults | **Multiplayer** = Yes (Online)
Developer = CD Projekt RED | **Genre** = RPG

Despite its awkward moniker, developer CD Projekt Red has made quite a name for itself over the years. It's not just a master of the RPG genre; it's a pioneer. And after years of pushing back the boundaries of what is possible with The Witcher series, CD Projekt Red has finally stretched its wings with a brand new IP. It's called, Cyberpunk 2077.

All the things we've come to love about The Witcher series can be found in Cyberpunk 2077, only bigger, better and deeper. Immense scale, complex characters, intense combat, a morally ambiguous story, engaging progression and breathtaking visuals all unfolding in a massive world.

As you've no doubt guessed, the game is set in the future; 2077 to be exact. There's been an apocalypse of sorts, but not as you might expect. Society has fallen to pieces and the world is controlled by megacorporations. These companies rule the metropolis from their skyscrapers, influencing everyone below them, right down to those living in the sewers.

It's down there with the rats that you start; basically a nobody trying to make sense of a world where drugs, sex, gangs and poverty blend with pop culture into a neon landscape. You've decided to shun the fake world perpetrated by the corporations and instead use cybernetics to enhance your body so you can try and make a name for yourself as a mercenary.

What's great about this game is the way your character, and your impact on the world, evolves in unscripted ways as you play. Epic story sequences – which include a cameo from Keanu Reeves of all people – offer branching dialogue paths. While a stack of different ability skill trees will see you finetune your playstyle as you go. Will you be a straight-up fighter, a hacker, someone who focusses on stealth, or a unique mix of the lot?

Combat is fast and frantic; as smooth as you might expect from a Call of Duty. But you don't always have to fight, using your other abilities and the open-ended nature of each area to find other ways to achieve your goals. If you can think of it, chances are you can do it.

This is top tier, true blockbuster gaming. It may be an RPG at heart, but it's got the combat to satisfy any action fan, and the exploration and visuals to keep adventure lovers' eyes glued to the screen. Worth getting!

DEMON'S SOULS REMAKE

Age Range = Adults | **Multiplayer** = Yes (Online)
Developer = From Software / Bluepoint Games | **Genre** = Action-RPG

One of the surprise PS5 launch titles – an exclusive, too – is a remake of beloved 2009 action-RPG Demon's Souls. The game is iconic for ushering in a new sub-genre of gaming where difficulty is welcomed. This is a tough game, requiring you to stay on edge and always paying attention. The medieval world is loaded with traps that will kill you in an instant. While combat requires measured and controlled real-time movement, parries and attacks. It's a game that demands that you fail, seek to improve yourself, and then comeback for more.

If you're willing to give yourself over to this style of play, which goes against the grain of most modern experiences, you'll find an immersive opus. One filled with haunting, atmospheric environments and challenging (sometimes huge) enemies that'll truly test you. The multiplayer mode in the original game was perhaps its only weak point, but thankfully that's been cleaned up and improved, too, now allowing for six people to fight it out to the death.

DESTRUCTION ALLSTARS

Age Range = All | **Multiplayer** = Yes (Local and Online)
Developer = Lucid Games | **Genre** = Racing Combat

Captured on PS5

There's no Twisted Metal announced for PS5, but there is a vehicular combat exclusive in Destruction AllStars. You jump into a futuristic arena and behind the wheel of a car armed with over-the-top weapons. You then try to take down your opponents. There are 16 different AllStars to choose from, each with their own unique rides to try out.

This game does differentiate itself from others in the genre after your car is destroyed. The game is not over at this point. Instead you find yourself on foot, trying to dodge those still racing around in vehicles while finding other ways of destroying them. Thankfully, once you're on your feet you get access to another run of abilities unique to your character to help you hang in there.

You can play the game solo, but this is definitely best played online. Sadly, the game was delayed to February 2021 just before launch.

DIRT 5

Age Range = All | **Multiplayer** = Yes (Local and Online)
Developer = Codemasters | **Genre** = Racing

When it comes to the racing genre, Codemasters is king. Its Dirt series, which focuses on all the off-road disciplines, is not only particularly good fun, but makes great use of next-generation technology. After all, you've got a lot of trackside detail, dynamic weather effects, seasonal shifts, night races, detailed car models, spectacular crash effects and dirt spluttering about everywhere. Plenty to put next-gen horsepower to good use.

Yet it's the gameplay that makes the series standout, not its amazing visuals. It's definitely not an arcade experience, but it's not quite a sim either. Instead it offers a control style that's accessible, yet offers plenty of room for improvement. Where you can master the art of driving a vehicle on a knife's edge. And there's no shortage of vehicles to try either, spanning a range of different classes.

Diversity is key with Dirt 5. The career mode has been revamped with a genuine story you can follow that leads you on a non-linear path down a host of different championship experiences. You can expect to go ice racing, enjoy stadium sprint cars, stampedes through forests, rallycrosses, off-road buggies and Gymkhana.

But it's worth noting that traditional point-to-point rallies aren't really a focus here – the Dirt Rally series is where you can find that experience.

You'll make your way around the globe as you go. USA (Arizona and New York City), Brazil, Morocco, China, Italy and Norway all offer up locations for you to race through. And you can do it offline or online.

Speaking of multiplayer, Dirt 5 gets extra points for offering local splitscreen gaming on the PS5. In fact, up to four friends can gather on the same couch to play Dirt 5, with both co-op and competitive experience on offer. It helps seal this title as one of the launch window's stand out games.

FIFA 21

Age Range = All | **Multiplayer** = Yes (Local and Online)
Developer = EA Sports | **Genre** = Sports

If you're looking for a game that can deliver endless hours of great fun either solo or with a friend, FIFA 21 is hard to ignore. The series needs little introduction, housing most of the top teams and leagues from around the world.

Every mode you can think of is on the table, including the famed Ultimate Team and a Career where you can play as a manager. There's even a story mode and a street football experience called Volta. It's a huge, huge game.

There's been the usual finetuning for the latest edition. For example, in the Career Mode there is deeper transfer and training management, as well as the ability to jump in and out of simulated matches as you please. The Ultimate Team mode now has a co-op feature, where you and a friend can compete together in squad battles.

The Volta street football mode returns with more locations, moves and tricks moves, too.

On the gameplay front, expect more dribbling control in one-on-one encounters. AI controlled players will make smarter moves to get into better positions, too. And thankfully you can control where another player runs just after you pass the ball to help them better get to the right spot. There are more realistic collisions and you have better control over the direction of headers.

At the time of writing, FIFA 21 hadn't been officially marked as a PS5 title, but you can upgrade to a PS5 version of the game if you buy the PS4 title for no cost. So it must be a PS5 title, right?

FORTNITE

Age Range = Teen | **Multiplayer** = Yes (Local and Online)
Developer = Epic Games | **Genre** = Battle Royale

Unless you've been hiding behind your bed with your fingers in your ears (you wouldn't be the first parent to do that!) you will have heard of Fortnite. The online shooter is a cultural phenomenon and for good reason. It's a really well-made, fun experience. And while it does involve shooting, it's done with colour and flair and over-the-top silliness, rather than blood and guts, making it good for younger gamers.

A huge amount of the game is free, but your kids will nag you about spending money for cosmetic enhancements to their character (which are endless). They don't need it, however. There's more to just the shooting, too. There's a full tournament mode, big social community and a creative mode that allows kids to bring their imaginations to life. It's constantly being updated, meaning every few months the whole experience becomes fresh again.

GODFALL

Age Range = Teen | **Multiplayer** = Yes (Online)
Developer = Counterplay Games | **Genre** = Action-RPG

A PS5 exclusive, Godfall has an intriguing premise. It's set in a high fantasy world on the brink of an apocalypse. You play as one of the last of the Knight's Order, charged with stopping the impending disaster either alone, or with up to two friends via drop-in, drop-out co-op. There is roleplay to be had in gathering as a team, with five different armour types and weapon classes defining your abilities and therefore how you can approach battle strategies.

Moment-to-moment gameplay unfolds like a third-person looter shooter, where you're forever seeking out better gear from felled enemies and levelling-up what your hero can unleash. However, it's all based on fast-paced, melee combat. Think of God of War and you'll have a good idea of what to expect. When combined with the fantasy setting, which crosses five realms - Earth, Water, Air, Fire and Spirit – you have a striking multiplayer launch title.

IMMORTALS FENYX RISING

Age Range = All | **Multiplayer** = No
Developer = Ubisoft Quebec | **Genre** = Action-Adventure

Launching a few weeks after the PS5, Immortals Fenyx Rising is Ubisoft's take on the brilliant open-world adventure experience offered by Nintendo's Legend of Zelda: Breath of the World. Played from the third-person perspective, you venture through a massive land filled with exotic beasts, challenging enemies, puzzles, ruins and different biomes based on Ancient Greek mythology. It even features a stunning cel-shaded visual style.

The story challenges your customisable character to rescue the Greek gods from an evil titan called Typhon. As you go you will unlock the tools you need to become a hero and there's no doubting how much the game takes its lead from Zelda. Gliding, horse riding, swimming, ranged combat with a bow and arrow, and melee attacks are ticked off the Zelda checklist. But it's hard to complain about getting access to such an experience outside of a Nintendo console!

MADDEN NFL 21

Age Range = All | **Multiplayer** = Yes (Local and Online)
Developer = EA Tiburon | **Genre** = Sports

Much like FIFA 21, EA has its other beloved sports series also ready and raring to go for next generation consoles. And like FIFA, while you will find improvements to the gameplay, it is not a full overhaul of the game to make use of the new power at hand. Don't expect any innovation here on what you've played before. That evolution will likely need to wait until Madden NFL 22.

In-game, playing against your friends or the AI, the gameplay remains fantastic fun. There's even an exciting new mode in The Yard, which is like a backyard, six-on-six version of the sport that rewards improvised play rather than set attacking strategies. It does this by adding unusual rule tweaks that keep players on their toes.

Elsewhere, only the Face of the Franchise mode, where you follow a story as a single player, has seen any significant update. Everything else has been left to stagnate for a year.

MANEATER

Age Range = Adults | **Multiplayer** = No
Developer = Tripwire Interactive | **Genre** = Action-RPG

Ever wanted to try life as a shark? It's awesome! This unique open-world action game sees you begin life as a baby bull shark looking to eat your way up the food chain, evolving as you go until you become a terrifying beast capable of taking down whole boats and the people on them. Effectively, you become Jaws.

Tripwire has done a great job not just creating large, open-water environments to explore, but also in making the shark control in a way that's both immersive and fun. It's all played with tongue-in-cheek, too, with your shark having some preposterous moves. You can throw scuba divers in the air with your jaws and tail whip them, for example. Or use a swordfish as a spear.

There's no doubt the game is brutally gory, but there's something ridiculously cathartic about eating your way through a world and pushing your shark against ever more challenging threats; which ultimately incudes gun-totting humans. Whacky yes, but a story worth diving into.

MARVEL'S SPIDER-MAN: MILES MORALES

Age Range = Teen | **Multiplayer** = No
Developer = Insomniac Games | **Genre** = Action-Adventure

The biggest exclusive game of the PS5 launch is Spider-Man: Miles Morales. The first Spider-Man, released in 2018, was a hit. Its gorgeous, open-world New York and movie-like story sequences were joined by some of the most enjoyable and fluid combat we've ever experienced. You truly felt like Spidey!

This follow-up isn't a true sequel as it's cut from the same cloth; it's built in the same game engine. However, it does offer a full new story experience. This time around you're in control of Miles Morales, another citizen bit by a genetically enhanced spider and then trained by Peter Parker to use his abilities. Miles must find a way to become his own hero by protecting his home neighbourhood of Harlem from the evil Tinkerer without derailing his mother's political career.

MORTAL KOMBAT 11 ULTIMATE

Age Range = Adult | **Multiplayer** = Yes (Local and Online)
Developer = NetherRealm Studios | **Genre** = Fighting

An Ultimate edition of 2019 fighting game Mortal Kombat 11 brings with it all the chaos and carnage the series has been famous for over the last few decades. For those unfamiliar with the series, two fighters face off in a 2D arena, unleashing a barrage of attacks, counters and special moves on each other until only one fighter is left.

Adding to the returning Fatalities and Brutalities are new Fatal Blows and Krushing Blows, as well as character customisation options. This Ultimate edition comes with the original game, two DLC packs and the Aftermath expansion. The latter adding a whole second story to follow. The DLC packs also build on the huge roster of original characters with some fun cameos, including Terminator, Joker and Robocop, plus the all new Rambo (voiced by Stallone himself).

A great game for local multiplayer, especially when both players are equally skilled.

MXGP 2020

Age Range = All | **Multiplayer** = Yes (Online)
Developer = Milestone | **Genre** = Racing

Developer Milestone is a racing specialist when it comes to two-wheels. They're behind the MotoGP, Monster Energy Supercross 3 and Ride series, as well as the official game of the MXGP championship. With the pandemic causing havoc with the 2020 season, this game has become an important way for fans to stay connected with the sport.

You'll find all 68 official riders and 19 official tracks in the game. You can also choose to create and customise your own rider and take them through the championship in pursuit of glory. The track editor returns, too, and has a much-welcomed addition in elevation. You no longer have to stick to flat tracks!

Also adding depth is the Race Director mode where you can create your own rules and race conditions, and an open-world Playground mode that lets you run amuck in the mountains of Norway. Great to look at and mechanically sound, MXGP is dirty in all the right ways.

NBA 2K21

Age Range = All | **Multiplayer** = Yes (Local and Online)
Developer = Visual Concepts | **Genre** = Sports

Over the years, the NBA titles from publisher 2K Games have been a great place to check out a new console's power at launch. So it is again with the PS5. It's fair to say the series has been close to photorealistic for years now, but the step-up in player likeness on the PS5 is jaw-dropping. While the faster framerate allows the intricate animations and crisp gameplay to really shine.

There's no shortage of teams to play, with all the NBA and WNBA sides included, as well as 67 classic teams from yesteryear. There's also the ability to customise and create six teams of your own, which can be fully integrated into the MyLeague and MyGM modes. The customisation gets deep in MyCareer, too, right down to haircuts and tattoos. Plus, you can now train and run drills to improve your player's attributes.

There are some valid complaints among fans that the series has started to stagnate, but it's still the best simulation of the sport in gaming.

OBSERVER: SYSTEM REDUX

Age Range = Adult | **Multiplayer** = No
Developer = Bloober Team | **Genre** = Horror

Most games set in the future are keen to show off a glittering new world full of futuristic gadgets. Not so much Observer. Set in Poland,

2086, you play an Observer; a special police unit tasked with watching over the thousands of survivors of a digital war who are sequestered into government housing having turned to drugs and crime. You're armed with the ability to hack into their minds as well as identify electronic devices and biological matter in the environment.

Things go pear-shaped when you discover your estranged son is among these oppressed people and somehow linked to a heinous crime. As you search for evidence and hack into people's mind, the story shifts in engaging and often terrifying ways. The game isn't big on combat, but instead puzzle-solving and psychology. The hacking sequences will really have you on edge, making this one of the PS5's more atmospheric launch offerings.

PATHLESS, THE

Age Range = All | **Multiplayer** = No
Developer = Giant Squid | **Genre** = Action-Adventure

The Pathless is a PS5 exclusive created by the same minds behind indie hit Abzû. It's not a game about big explosions and endless bullets, but is instead a spiritual and atmospheric exploration game with a auto-runner twist.

You play as the Hunter and your goal is to bring light to obelisks scattered around an island in order to remove a curse. To do this, you dash through the world with an eagle companion, using your bow and arrow to shoot talismans that in turn grant you the energy to keep your momentum moving forward.

It's an open world, but not in the traditional sense of following a map around. Instead you use Spirit Vision to identify areas of interest and then work out a way to reach them. This can involve being carried by the eagle when it's flying, with the bird upgradable as you go depending on how many crystals you collect.

You can walk about, but you must keep moving. The entire time, you are chased by invisible cursed spirts, and if they get you, they'll rob you of all the crystals you have collected. If you can't see a way to escape, you can resort to stealth, trying to stay hidden and quiet until the threat passes.

As you may have guesses, The Pathless is a rather unique playing experience. Shooting your arrows is more based on timing than accuracy, helping to create a fluid movement experience that's almost musical. The visual style is cartoony, but not in a kiddy way. And even though the island is shrouded in mugginess, when you get up high – carried in the claws of your companion – there is definitely a sense of scale to enjoy.

If you're looking for something different to enjoy at the PS5's launch, and don't mind indie game experiences that look to wow with atmosphere, then give The Pathless a try.

PLANET COASTER: CONSOLE EDITION

Age Range = All | **Multiplayer** = No
Developer = Frontier Developments | **Genre** = Sandbox

Do you remember Theme Park from the 1990s? Or more recently the Rollercoaster Tycoon series? This game follows in their footsteps, tasking you with constructing a massive theme park and then managing its operation. Whether you look to do that through the campaign with limited funds and quests to complete, or choose to go into the Sandbox mode with unlimited coin allowing your imagination to go nuts, it's a great time sink for any agile mind.

What's most impressive about this game over others in the genre is the creation tools. You don't just select a rollercoaster from a menu and place it on your land. You can really dive in and place each track, giving it a unique feel and look via a huge array of options. Naturally you can ride your amusements once complete, but you can also share your creations online with the world. A game of huge depth.

SACKBOY: A BIG ADVENTURE

Age Range = All | **Multiplayer** = Yes (Local and Online)
Developer = Sumo Digital | **Genre** = Platformer

You may recognise Sackboy as the star of the LittleBigPlanet series. This is indeed a spin-off to that title, but it plays completely differently.

Rather than a 2D platformer with a focus on creation, this is a 3D adventure focused on play. It's more like a Mario title, although it does retain the great four-player co-op experience of its predecessor.

The worlds you explore are truly gorgeous. It looks like every element has been hand-crafted and you'll be hard-pressed to find a pixel that doesn't offer some spectacular detail or activity. The controls are easy to master, too, while leveraging the strengths of the DualSense.

Sackboy himself comes equipped with new moves, but the gameplay in truth doesn't veer far from the collecting, puzzle-solving, obstacle-dodging and simplistic combat for which the genre is known. And there's absolutely nothing wrong with that!

WATCH DOGS: LEGION

Age Range = Adults | **Multiplayer** = Yes (Online)
Developer = Ubisoft Toronto | **Genre** = Action-Adventure

If you've come across the Watch Dogs series before, you'll know it's set in a future dystopian where the government is always watching. You play a hacker looking to stay in the shadows, using your hacking skills to subvert the system and manipulate the world and its people into helping you bring "the man" down.

Watch Dogs: Legion sticks to that core goal, but takes us to a gorgeous, fictionalised London – albeit one full of recognisable landmarks. The third-person gameplay, with its mix of melee and weapon-based combat, parkour movement and stealth mechanics, also remains in place.

Other than a bigger world with more skills to unlock and utilise there is one major change to the gameplay. By using your reputation in the hacker group DedSec and completing missions, you can recruit new members. You can then switch to play as those new members, utilising their strengths based on the mission you need to complete. The bad news is, if you die that character is lost, with you transporting into the skin of one of your other recruits.

There's also plenty to enjoy on the multiplayer front, even though early adopters must wait till December 2020 for the modes to become available.

The highlight is the ability to team up in the campaign with three friends in four-player co-op. However, there's also a Tactical Ops mode full of dedicated co-op missions, as well as a Spiderbot Arena competitive mode. The asymmetrical multiplayer feature called Invasion also returns, whereby you can enter someone else's game world and stalk them.

If you were a fan of the Mr. Robot TV series, this game should definitely catch your attention.

WORMS RUMBLE

Age Range = All | **Multiplayer** = Yes (Online)
Developer = Team 17 | **Genre** = Action

No game series has provided as many laugh-out-loud moments as Worms. Put a bunch of worms in a randomly generated environment stacked with pitfalls and booby traps, and then arms those worms with a huge arsenal of weapons that range from standard military affair to truly bizarre concepts, and you're going to giggle!

PS5 gamers get exclusive first access to the new Worms Rumble game, which retains the 2D perspective we know and love, but dramatically changes up the gameplay. Rather than turn-based combat, the action now unfolds in real-time. While the number of players has been upped to 32, ensuring true chaos in the core deathmatch or battle royale modes.

The level destruction is gone as a result of this new approach to retain the integrity of the level during a match, but it's still a great new way to experience this series.

WHAT DOES THE FUTURE LOOK LIKE FOR PS5?

There's plenty to look forward to with Sony's PlayStation 5. From a hardware perspective, we should eventually see a PSVR 2.0 headset and improved Move controllers, adding a whole other dimension to the play experience on the console. We'll also likely see a PS5 Pro model a few years down the track offering even more power and a bigger internal hard drive.

Most of the excitement can be drawn from the list of upcoming games. Sony has announced a run of blockbuster franchise returns in 2021 and beyond. This includes **Gran Turismo 7** from Polyphony Digital, **Ratchet & Clank: Rift Apart**, the exciting sequel **Horizon Forbidden West** (pictured) and even **God of War: Ragnarok**.

There's obviously a tonne of other killer franchises in the Sony stable that may reappear, too. Uncharted, The Last of Us, Jak & Daxter, Twisted Metal, Everybody's Golf, Ape Escape, Killzone, Resistance,

LittleBigPlanet, SOCOM, Sly Cooper, SingStar, MediEvil, MotorStorm, Infamous, Wipeout, Knack and plenty more could all get sequels.

Third-party developers are also on board in a big way. The next game from Dishonored creator Arkane Studios is called **Deathloop** and it's a timed PS5 exclusive. As is **GhostWire: Tokyo** by the creator of The Evil Within and Resident Evil series, and a new title from RPG maestros Square Enix called **Project Athia**.

Exclusive science-fiction psychological horror game **Returnal** from Housemarque also looks exciting, as does the next entry in the Oddworld series, **Oddworld: Soulstorm**.

Elsewhere, the best of the multiformat blockbusters have PS5 earmarked as part of their release strategy. There are too many exciting titles to mention here, but I will throw out some early highlights for 2021 just to whet your appetite.

- Balan Wonderworld
- Chorus
- Far Cry 6
- Gotham Knights
- Hitman 3
- Hood: Outlaws & Legends
- Jett: The Far Shore
- Kena: Bridge of Spirits
- Lord of the Rings: Gollum, The
- Marvel's Avengers
- Outriders
- Resident Evil Village
- Tom Clancy's Rainbow Six Quarantine

That list alone should get you pumped for the years ahead!

ALSO OUT

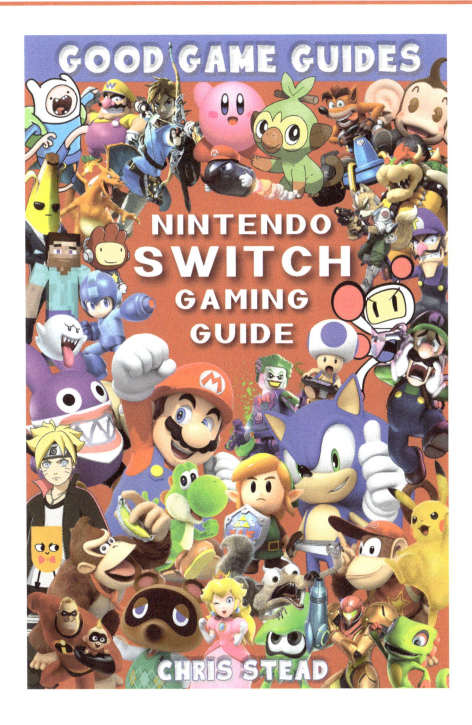

Lightning Source UK Ltd.
Milton Keynes UK
UKHW021328171221
395775UK00001B/23